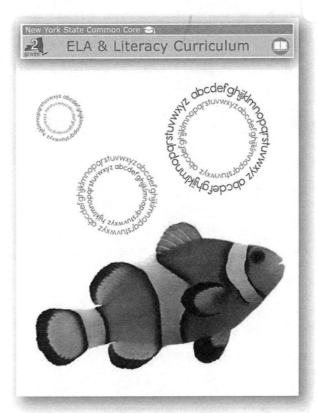

Unit 4
Workbook

Skills Strand
GRADE 2

Core Knowledge Language Arts®
New York Edition

Core Knowledge®

Unit 4
Workbook

    This Workbook contains worksheets that accompany many of the lessons from the Teacher Guide for Unit 4. Some of the worksheets in this book do not include written instructions for the student because the instructions would have contained nondecodable words. The expectation is that teachers will explain these worksheets to the students orally, using the guidelines in the Teacher Guide. The Workbook is a student component, which means that each student should have a Workbook.

Dear Family Member,

We will start a new unit this week. The Reader for this unit is *The Job Hunt*. In this book, Kim, a college student, hunts for a job. Her younger brother, Kurt, follows along as she goes from place to place in her search. Kim and Kurt will visit many places in New York City as they ride the subway and walk to each location.

Please continue to try to find time to read with your child daily. We encourage you to take advantage of the public library so your child can select books of interest. The librarian should be able to direct you to books appropriate for most second graders. It is fine for your child to occasionally choose books that may be too hard for her/him to read independently. For example, if your child is interested in horses, she may select a book with many interesting photographs of horses, but it may be too difficult to read alone. Encourage your child to talk to you about the illustrations and to try to read whatever he or she can, while you assist with more difficult words.

The following are the spelling words for this week. We have already learned how to read words with these sounds in other lessons earlier this year. For example, your child has learned the /aw/ sound may be spelled either 'aw' or 'au', the /oi/ sound may be spelled either as 'oi' or 'oy', and the /oo/ sound, as in *moon*, can be spelled several different ways.

Remember when you practice with your child during the week, call out the words in random order to make sure he/she has really learned each word.

hawk	vault	oil	cowboy	moon
yawn	haunted	spoiled	enjoy	spool
crawl	causes	coin	destroy	cartoon

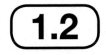
Yes or No?

1. Can a dog chirp with joy? _____

2. Can yogurt sing as you eat it? _____

3. Can birds perch on a tree branch? _____

4. Do squirrels have gray fur? _____

5. Do you like to stir dirt into your milk? _____

6. Would your mom be pleased if you burped out loud at dinner?
   _____

7. Could a nurse place a thermometer in your mouth?
   _____

8. Can you draw a pattern on your paper? _____

9. Can a clown be part of a circus? _____

10. If you use sunblock, could you still get a sunburn? _____

11. Could your purse eat popcorn? _____

12. Would a glass of sawdust take away your thirst? _____

13. Can a waitress serve us lunch after she takes our order?

    _____

14. Is Thursday a day in the weekend? _____

15. Could you surf in the desert? _____

16. Can you cook hamburgers on a grill? _____

17. Can you make a cake in a whirlpool? _____

18. Can a girl turn and turn to make her skirt twirl?

    _____

19. Can a girl with short hair have curls? _____

20. Can you jump feet first into a pool? _____

21. Can a curb be at the side of the road? _____

Yes (Same) or No (Different)?

Directions: Have students read each pair of words and decide if the vowel sounds are the same. Have students write yes if the sounds are the same or no if the sounds are different.

1.   third – thorn   _____

2.   nurse – clerk   _____

3.   bird – burn   _____

4.   chirp – church   _____

5.   skirt – shirt   _____

6.   fur – far   _____

7.   surf – sir   _____

8.   burst – barn   _____

9.   prize – purse   _____

10. Carl – curl   _____

11. hurt – girl   _____

12. skirt – dirt   _____

13. verb – herd   _____

14. Burt – Bert _____

15. perk – park _____

16. fir – fur _____

17. curve – churn _____

18. fern – curb _____

19. stir – turn _____

20. thorn – bore _____

Mixed Review R-Controlled Vowels

Dear Family Member,

Ask your child to read each sentence and the two word choices. Your child should write the best choice for each sentence in the blank.

1. _____ and Kim are job hunting.
   (Kurt   Corn)

2. Jill would like to get three more _____.
   (skirts   swirls)

3. A bird will _____ to its mom for food.
   (curb   chirp)

4. Did you _____ a log in the fireplace?
   (burn   burst)

5. A _____ can help you when you are hurt.
   (purse   nurse)

6. Did you see the boy as he _____ the huge
   (surfed   barked)
   waves?

7. Beth asked her mom to help _____ her hair.
   (churn   curl)

8. Would you rather put on a red or a green _____?
   (shirt   fork)

9. Who was your teacher in _____ grade?
   (fire   first)

10. The _____ dug holes next to the tree to hide
(sunburn   squirrel)
acorns.

11. The _____ is herding the sheep.
(artist   shepherd)

12. Did you _____ that today is my birthday?
(target   forget)

Yes (Same) or No (Different)?

Part I: Does the letter 'y' have the same sound in each word pair?

1. yelp – myth _____

2. gym – myth _____

3. Lynn – yarn _____

4. yikes – lynx _____

5. Syd – gym _____

Part II: Do these words have the same vowel sound?

1. join – gym _____

2. miss – myth _____

3. gym – jam _____

4. myth – math _____

5. quill – lynx _____

Fill in the Blank

Write the best word from the box in the blank to finish each sentence.

cymbals	synonyms	oxygen	gym
~~cylinder~~	myths	symbol	antonym

1. A can is __cylinder__ shaped.

2. I exercise at the _____.

3. When the boy in the band clapped the _____ together, they made a loud sound like a gong.

4. An _____ of the word "yes" is the word "no."

5. In math problems, a "+" is the _____ telling you to add the numbers.

6. "Smile" and "grin" have the same meaning and are _____.

7. The teacher read the class some Greek _____.

8. Humans breathe _____.

Brooklyn

Kim took Kurt by the hand and the two of them set off so that Kim could look for a job.

It was a summer morning in Brooklyn. There were lots of cars on the streets. There were people walking here and there. A man was sweeping the street outside his shop.

Kim and Kurt walked until they got to Prospect Park.

Kurt looked into the park as they went past. He saw people playing frisbee. He saw people on bikes. He saw a man playing fetch with his dog. He saw soccer players on their way to a game. He saw runners on their way to the gym.

"Can we stop and play?" asked Kurt.

"No," Kim said. "I have to get a job."

Kurt slumped a bit to let Kim see that he was sad, but he kept walking.

"Kim," he said after a bit, "will having a job make you a grownup?"

"Well, sort of," said Kim. "I'm in college. I think that makes me part kid and part grownup."

"Will you still have time to play with me?"

"Yes!" Kim said, rubbing Kurt's arm. "We will have lots of time to play. I'll get a part-time job, one that is not too hard. That way, I will not be too tired when I get home. Then we can play."

"You should get a job at the Bronx Zoo!" Kurt said. "Then you can play with the snakes and tigers."

Kim said. "I don't think so. I don't like snakes. But we can visit the zoo later this summer. After I get a job, I will have cash to do fun things like that."

Just then Kim saw two old pals waving at her.

"Lynn!" she yelled. "Sheryl! What's up?"

Lynn and Sheryl crossed the street. "Hi, Kim!" said Lynn. "Are you home from college for the summer?"

"Yes," said Kim. "It's good to be back here in Brooklyn!"

Kim slapped hands with her pals. Then she said, "You two have met Kurt, haven't you?"

Lynn and Sheryl nodded. Lynn stooped down to look at Kurt and said, "Hi, big man! Would you like to come with us? We are going over to Drummer's Grove to see the drummers."

"Drummer's Grove?" Kurt said. "Can we go, Kim? Can we? Can we? Can we?"

Kim was not sure what to say. She needed to get started on her job hunt. But she wanted Kurt to have fun, too. If she dragged him off without seeing the drummers, there was a chance he would get mad and fuss all day. That would not be much fun.

"Okay," she said at last. "But just for a bit. I need to get started with my job hunt."

Brooklyn

1. Where are Kim and Kurt?

    Kim and Kurt are in _____.

    A. Manhattan

    B. Brooklyn

    C. Bronx

    D. Queens

2. When Kim and Kurt get to Prospect Park, what does Kurt want to do?

    Kurt wants to _____.

    A. eat ice cream

    B. go to the gym

    C. look for a job

    D. stop and play

3. Why is Kurt sad?

    Kurt is sad because _____.

    A. Kim says he cannot get ice cream

    B. Kim says Kurt must look for a job

    C. Kim says that they cannot stop and play

    D. Kim says Kurt must go home

4. Why is Kim looking for a part-time job?
   Kim wants to have time to _____.

   A. read books for college

   B. play and do fun things with Kurt

   C. sleep late each morning

   D. exercise at the gym

5. Where do Lynn and Sheryl invite Kim and Kurt to go?
   They invite Kim and Kurt to go with them to _____.

   A. the Bronx Zoo

   B. Brooklyn

   C. Queens

   D. Drummer's Grove

Circle the name of the character who made the statement.

Sentence	Character			
"I think that makes me part kid and part grownup."	Kurt	Lynn	Kim	Sheryl
"You should get a job at the Bronx Zoo!"	Kurt	Lynn	Kim	Sheryl
"Hi, big man! Would you like to come with us?"	Kurt	Lynn	Kim	Sheryl

Fill in the Blank

kind	entire	finish	pilot	find
child	mind	surprise	grind	wild

1.   A cat is tame and can be a pet, but a tiger is _____.

2.   What _____ of ice cream do you like the best?

3.   Lynn hid my notebook and now I cannot _____ it.

4.   The _____ landed the plane on time.

5.   A _____ cannot drive a car.

6.   The farmer will _____ the wheat into flour.

7.   Don't tell Kim what I got for her birthday. I want to _____ her.

8.   The teacher said we had to _____ the math problems before we could go outside.

9.   Do you _____ if I sit next to you?

10. Bill ate the _____ pie and then felt sick!

Write 5 sentences telling why "Drummer's Grove" is a good title for this story.

_____

_____

_____

_____

_____

_____

_____

_____

_____

_____

Spelling Test

1. _____

2. _____

3. _____

4. _____

5. _____

6. _____

7. _____

8. _____

9. _____

10. _____

11. _____

12. _____

13. _____

14. _____

15. _____

_____

 _____

_____

Synonyms and Antonyms

Write the best word from the box on the line to finish each sentence.

sigh	night	~~frighten~~	high
right	light	fight	

1. A synonym of "scare" is "___frighten___."

   A witch could ___frighten___ a child.

2. An antonym of "day" is "_____."

   We sleep during the _____.

3. An antonym of "wrong" is "_____."

   Bill got all of his spelling words _____ on the test.

4. An antonym of "dark" is "_____."

   Please turn on the _____ so I can read.

5. A synonym of "argue" is "_____."

   When my sister and I do not agree, we _____.

6. A synonym for "puff" is "_____."

   Bart let out a _____ when his dad said to turn off the TV.

7. A synonym for "tall" is "_____."

   I cannot reach the box because it is on a _____ shelf.

Synonyms and Antonyms

Write the best word from the box on the line to finish each sentence.

highway	tight	flight
upright	bright	might

8. A synonym for "may" is "_____."

    I _____ not go to soccer today because I feel sick.

9. An antonym of "dim" is "_____."

    I needed sunglasses because it was so _____ outside.

10. A synonym for a "plane trip" is "_____."

    My _____ was late, so I did not get there on time.

11. An antonym of "loose" is "_____."

    My pants are too _____.

12. A synonym of "road" is "_____."

    We will take the _____ to drive to the store.

13. A synonym of "standing" is "_____."

    The chair on the deck tipped over during the storm, so I
    turned it back _____.

Dwight's Lights

1. What is printed on the poster in Dwight's Lights?

    A.   "Sale!" is printed on the poster.

    B.   "Open!" is printed on the poster.

    C.   "Dwight is hiring!" is printed on the poster.

    Page _____

2. Why is Dwight's Lights so bright?

    A.   The shop has a lot of sun.

    B.   The shop has hundreds of lights and lamps, all of which
         are on.

    C.   The shop is on fire.

    Page _____

3. Dwight is very loud with Kim and Kurt. Why?

    A.   Dwight would like to sell a light or lamp to Kim and
         Kurt.

    B.   Dwight is mad at Kim and Kurt.

    C.   There is a lot of noise in the shop.

    Page _____

Directions: Have students reread the story and answer the questions.

4. Why is it that Dwight's face falls when Kim says that she has no need for a light?

   A.   Dwight had hoped to make a sale and get some cash.

   B.   Dwight is feeling ill.

   C.   Dwight would like to spend some more time with Kim and Kurt.

   Page _____

5. Do you think that you would like Dwight? Why or why not?

   _____

   _____

   _____

   _____

   _____

   _____

Dear Family Member,

This week all of the spelling words contain r-controlled vowels. You may also notice the number of spelling words each week has increased. We are beginning to step up the rigor of our program as students become more adept at reading and spelling words.

In addition to reading every night for at least 20 minutes, students should practice spelling words.

As always, if you have questions or concerns, please do not hesitate to contact me.

/ar/	/or/	/er/		
'ar'	'or'	'er'	'ir'	'ur'
car	store	nerve	stir	fur
bar	chore	serve	shirt	hurt
			girl	turn
			bird	purse

Tricky Word: all

Fill in the Blank

Part I

1.   one dragonfly, three _____

2.   one butterfly, three _____

3.   one firefly, three _____

4.   one spy, three _____

Part II

1.   cry _____

2.   fly _____

3.   dry _____

4.   try _____

5.   multiply _____

Directions: Have students practice changing 'y' to 'i' and adding –es to each word. Refer to the Teacher Guide, Lesson 6 for detailed directions.

Part III

1. A _____ is fast.
    (dragonfly)

2. I caught a jar of _____.
    (firefly)

3. There were lots of _____ in the tree.
    (butterfly)

4. The dress _____ as it hangs in the sun.
    (dry)

5. When I haven't had something to eat for a while, a hamburger _____ my hunger.
    (satisfy)

Part I:

1. The _____ went fishing at the lake.
   plural of "man"

   A. mans

   B. men

   C. mens

2. The _____ enjoyed playing checkers.
   plural of "child"

   A. childs

   B. children

   C. childrens

3. Bart went home to get some boots when it started to rain so his _____ would stay dry.
   plural of "foot"

   A. foots

   B. feets

   C. feet

Directions: Part I: Have students circle the letter of the best answer for each sentence.

Unit 4   29
© 2013 Core Knowledge Foundation

4. The dentist cleaned my _____.
   plural of "tooth"

   A. teeth

   B. teeths

   C. toothes

5. I saw _____ flying up in the sky.
   plural of "goose"

   A. gooses

   B. geeses

   C. geese

6. The cat was chasing three _____.
   plural of "mouse"

   A. mouses

   B. mice

   C. mices

Part II:

man _____S_____   children _____

teeth _____P_____   fireflies _____

tooth _____   mice _____

geese _____   pencil _____

dishes _____   feet _____

Fill in the Blank

1. He _____ to bake a cake.
   (tribe   tries)

2. Can you tell if she _____ at sad tales?
   (cries   tribes)

3. The horse _____ at the gate.
   (shies   shy)

4. The _____ are in jail for stealing secrets.
   (shies   spies)

5. I like french _____ with my burger.
   (spies   fries)

6. Blue _____ with white clouds means a nice day.
   (flies   skies)

7. We must get _____ for our camping trip.
   (fireflies   supplies)

8. The teacher _____ large numbers with ease.
   (satisfies   multiplies)

9. Just one hamburger _____ my hunger.
   (satisfies   requires)

10. You can see _____ in the dark when they
    (butterflies   fireflies)
    light up on a summer's night.

Directions: Have students write the correct word in each blank.

Name _____

HELP WANTED:
Greeting Clerk

Need one person to help at local gym. Must be able to work 9 to 5 each day. Weekends off. Should be a good writer and speller. Must be nice and cheerful. Must like to work with people.

1. What and where is this job?

    _____
    _____
    _____

2. How many people are needed for this job?

    _____
    _____
    _____

3. What time would you have to start this job each day?

    _____
    _____

4. Will you have to be at the job on Saturday?

    _____
    _____
    _____

5. If you get this job, how should you act?

_____

_____

_____

6. What skills do you need to get this job?

_____

_____

_____

7. Why do you think a greeting clerk should be good at spelling and writing?

_____

_____

_____

8. Do you think a greeting clerk needs to know how to use the gym equipment?

_____

_____

_____

9. If you get this job, will you smile or frown? Why?

_____

_____

_____

Fill in the Blank

1. My sister is one year _____ today.
    (told   old)

2. A _____ of lightning hit the tree.
    (toll   bolt)

3. We had to pay a _____ to drive on the highway.
    (told   toll)

4. Would you like a dinner _____ with your meat?
    (scroll   roll)

5. Who has the _____ eggs in a basket?
    (told   most)

6. I have a stuffed up nose and a bad _____.
    (cold   gold)

7. Dad will _____ us if we don't do our jobs.
    (sold   scold)

8. Can you help me _____ the fence post while I
    (sold   hold)
    fix it?

9. Would you like to go for a _____ outside to get
    (colt   stroll)
    some exercise?

10. Will you help me _____ the clean shirts?
    (fold   sold)

Write a summary of what Kurt learned about diners in this story.

_____

_____

_____

_____

_____

_____

_____

_____

_____

_____

TAKE HOME

The Gym

After leaving Dwight's Lights, Kim stopped for a moment to think about where she should try next to find a job.

"Mom's pals, Tom and Beth, run a gym that is nearby, I might have a chance getting a job at their gym, so let's go!"

On the way to the gym, Kim explained to Kurt that a gym is a place where people go to exercise and get in shape. She explained that people pay to be members of a gym.

Kurt had never visited a gym. The gym seemed odd to him. He stood staring at a man who was jogging in place.

"He keeps running," said Kurt, "but he is still in the same place!"

"It's kind of like the wheel that rat of yours likes to run on," said Kim. "It lets him run in place."

"He's not a rat," said Kurt. "He's a hamster!"

Kurt kept on looking at the man jogging in place.

"Why not just run in the park?" he asked.

"Some people think the gym is fun, just like you think the park is fun," Kim said.

"All the people here are working hard," Kurt said. "Why do they pay to work so hard?"

"It makes them feel good and strong after they have finished," Kim said.

Just then Tom and Beth came over to see them.

"Hi, Kim! Hi, Kurt!" said Beth. "It's good to see you. What brings you here?"

Kim said, "I'm looking for a summer job. I stopped to see if you need help. Are you hiring?"

"We just hired someone for a job in the snack bar," Beth said, pointing over to the counter. "People like to have a cool drink and a snack when they finish in the gym."

"That looks like a good job," said Kim. "I wish I had gotten here sooner."

"Bad timing," said Beth. "We don't need more help right now. But you will find a job somewhere else."

Tom took Kurt and Kim to see the rest of the gym.

Kurt pointed at a man who was doing curls.

"What's he doing?" Kurt asked.

"He's doing curls," Tom explained. "Would you like to do some curls?"

Kurt nodded.

"Here," Tom said.

"Use this one. Lift it up. That will strengthen your biceps—the tops of your arms. Then let it down. That will strengthen your triceps—the backs of your arms."

Kurt did five or six curls. Then he clenched his arm and yelled, "I am the man of steel!"

Kim just smiled at Kurt.

Kim spoke to Beth and Tom. "Well, I suppose we should go," she said. "Thank you for meeting with me."

"No problem," said Tom.

"Good luck with the job hunt," said Beth. "We will send word to you if we need help here."

"Why don't you go see Alberto at the corner market?" added Tom. "He may have a job for you. Plus, he's one of the nicest men I have ever met."

The Gym

TAKE HOME

1. What is a gym?

_____

_____

_____

_____

2. Why do people pay to join a gym?

_____

_____

_____

_____

3. Who are Tom and Beth?

_____

_____

_____

_____

4. Why don't Tom and Beth hire Kim?

_____

_____

_____

5. What advice does Tom give Kim?

_____

_____

_____

6. What do you do to exercise?

_____

_____

_____

7. Would you rather run outside or run inside a gym? Why?

_____

_____

_____

blow	fowl	owl	glow	row
show	howl	slow	prowl	snow
tow	crown	grow	frown	gown
clown	throw	growl	scowl	town

/oe/ like *snow*   /ow/ like *now*

_____   _____

_____   _____

_____   _____

_____   _____

_____   _____

_____   _____

_____   _____

_____   _____

_____   _____

_____   _____

Directions: Have students read the words in the box aloud, circle the tricky spelling 'ow', and then sort the words into correct columns.

glow	snow	throw	gown	cloud
pound	sound	howl	town	crown

1. We have a house in a small _____.

2. Did you hear the _____ of the crickets?

3. Can you _____ a ball?

4. Fireflies can _____ in the dark at night.

5. Did you hear the dog _____ at the moon?

6. Sometimes when it is cold, _____ will fall and make the ground white.

7. Is there a _____ in the sky?

8. The queen has a _____.

9. The clerk at the market sold me a _____ of beans.

10. I like my pink _____ the most.

Spelling Test

1. _____   9. _____

2. _____   10. _____

3. _____   11. _____

4. _____   12. _____

5. _____   13. _____

6. _____   14. _____

7. _____   15. _____

8. _____

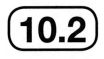

Singular and Plural Nouns

Singular Nouns (one)	Plural Nouns (more than one)
child	
butterfly	
man	
tooth	
class	
foot	
woman	
mouse	

Directions: Have students write the plural form of each noun on the corresponding line. Then have students make up two sentences using at least one of the plural nouns from the exercise in each sentence.

1. _____

   _____

   _____

2. _____

   _____

   _____

Singular and Plural Nouns

Part I

1. wife _____

2. loaf _____

3. elf _____

4. hoof _____

5. shelf _____

6. half _____

Part II

1. _____

   _____

   _____

2. _____

   _____

   _____

calves	scarf	loaves	leaf
leaves	halves	hoof	elves

1. When it is cold, Sheryl wears her red _____ wrapped around her neck.

2. The _____ on the trees turn red and yellow in the fall.

3. Mom cut the muffin into two _____ so that Bart and Jill each could have a part to eat.

4. Pam mixed flour, eggs, and milk to make three _____.

5. _____ help Santa each year.

6. I slipped on a wet _____ on the steps outside.

7. The _____ are in the barn with the cows.

8. The horse started to limp; so we looked and found a thorn in its _____.

The Subway

1. Where do Kim and Kurt need to go on the subway?

   _____

   _____

   _____

2. Will Kim and Kurt get to see the East River? Why or why not?

   _____

   _____

   _____

3. What is the meaning of the word "sub"?

   _____

   _____

   _____

4. Why does Kurt want to get off the train?

   _____

   _____

   _____

5. What happens at the Wall Street stop?

   _____

   _____

   _____

6. Have you ever taken a subway? If so, what was it like? If not, would you like to? Why or why not?

_____

_____

_____

First, number the sentences in the proper order. Then rewrite the sentences in the right order.

Kurt and Kim got seats on the train. _____

Kurt and Kim waited on the platform. _____

Kurt and Kim left the diner. _____

Kim grabbed a strap, and Kurt grabbed Kim's leg. _____

Kurt and Kim looked at the subway map. _____

1. _____

2. _____

3. _____

4. _____

5. _____

Dear Family Member,

This week's spelling words focus on the spelling 'ow', which can stand for two sounds as in "glow" or "now." On the back of this letter is a variation of the "I Spy" game you may have played with your child. It is called "I Am Thinking of a Word." You will provide clues to describe something about which you are thinking; your child should guess the correct word and write it as the answer. Your child may enjoy playing this game as a different way to practice these spelling words.

First, ask your child to read the entire list of spelling words. Then say each clue, asking your child to think of which spelling word you are describing and write the word.

below	yellow
elbow	rainbow
snow	sorrow
arrow	plow
flowers	growling
powder	shower
meow	chow

Tricky Word: your

Clues for "I Am Thinking of a Word" Game

1. I am thinking of a word that means the same thing as under. (below)

2. I am thinking of a word for a color. (yellow)

3. I am thinking of a word for a part of your arm. (elbow)

4. I am thinking of a word for something that may appear in the sky after it rains. (rainbow)

5. I am thinking of a word for something that is white and falls from the sky. (snow)

6. I am thinking of a synonym for sadness. (sorrow)

7. I am thinking of a word for something you shoot with a bow. (arrow)

8. I am thinking of a word for a tool a farmer might use to prepare the soil for planting a garden. (plow)

9. I am thinking of another word for blossom. (flowers)

10. I am thinking of a word for a sound a dog may make. (growling)

11. I am thinking of a word that is something you might put on a baby. (powder)

12. I am thinking of a word that describes a way you might get clean instead of taking a bath. (shower)

13. I am thinking of a word for a sound that a cat makes. (meow)

14. I am thinking of a word that is something a puppy might eat. (chow)

15. I am thinking of a word that means something belongs just to you. (your)

Fill in the Blank

athlete	beach	zebra	expect	fever	replied
else	second	became	pretend	create	decide

1. He is a good _____ and plays football for a pro team.

2. Sometimes my sister likes to wear a crown and a long dress and _____ that she is a princess.

3. When I asked my mom if I could stay up until midnight, she firmly _____, "No way!"

4. A _____ looks like a horse with black and white stripes.

5. He _____ a third grader at the beginning of the year.

6. On a summer day, I like to spend the day at the _____, relaxing and swimming.

7. Mark has a _____ and does not feel well.

8. Lynn came in first place in the race and Sheryl came in _____.

Family Member Directions: Have your child first read all the words in the box and then choose the best word from the box to complete each sentence.

Fill in the Blank

athlete	beach	zebra	expect	fever	replied
else	second	became	pretend	create	decide

9. Kurt had a hard time trying to _____ what kind of ice cream to order because he liked them all.

10. What time do you _____ your aunt to get here?

11. The artist will _____ a new painting to be displayed in the art show.

12. I have looked everywhere for my lost purse and don't know where _____ to search.

More Proper Nouns

Part I:

mr halter _____   miss burks _____

ms parker _____   mrs binns _____

miss jacks _____   mr hunt _____

mrs tripp _____   ms. sims _____

Part II:

girl _____   street _____

teacher _____   state _____

day _____   boy _____

1. do you know if bill sold the old truck to mr tucker last sunday

_____

_____

_____

_____

2. mrs fine tripped on the curb thursday at miss smith's house

_____

_____

_____

_____

Persuasive Writing Plan

Kind of persuasive writing: _____ Letter _____

1. Opening Sentence:

    _____

    _____

    _____

2. Reason:

    _____

    _____

    _____

3. Reason:

    _____

    _____

    _____

Directions: Have students use this template to plan a persuasive letter.

4. Reason:

_____

_____

_____

5. Closing Sentence:

_____

_____

_____

Persuasive Letter

_____

(School Street Address)

_____

(City, State, Zip Code)

_____

(Date)

Dear _____,
         (Principal's name)

_____

_____

_____

_____

_____

_____

_____

Sincerely,

_____

Directions: Have students use this template to draft a persuasive letter.

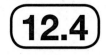

Editing Checklist
for Friendly Letter

Fill out this chart as you edit the draft.

1. Do I have a heading?	
2. Do I have a greeting?	
3. Do I have a body?	
4. Do I have a closing?	
5. Have I added my signature at the end?	
6. Do all of my sentences start with uppercase letters?	
7. Do all of my sentences end with a final mark? (. ? or !)	
8. Have I spelled all of my words correctly?	

The Subway

When Kim and Kurt were finished eating, Kim paid for the meal and left a tip for the waitress. Then they went out of the diner.

"We need to get on the subway and go into Manhattan," she said.

"Manhattan?" Kurt said with a loud sigh. "This job hunt will take all day!"

"It won't take that long. I'm just having no luck here in Brooklyn. Maybe I can find a job in Manhattan."

They walked to the subway stop.

Kim got out the fare card her mom had given her.

"Which train will we take?" Kurt asked.

"The Number 3 train."

Kim pointed to a map on the wall. She showed Kurt a red line on the map. "We will ride from here in Brooklyn over to Manhattan and all the way up to Times Square."

Kurt pointed at the spot on the map that marked the East River.

"Will we get to see the river?"

"No," said Kim. "The subway goes under the river. That's why it's named a subway. Sub means under. A subway is a train that goes under things like rivers and roads. It travels underground."

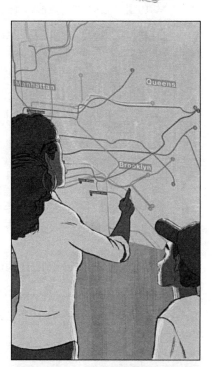

Kurt and Kim waited on the platform for the subway train. Soon, Kurt could hear the sound of the train as it got closer. There was a gust of air. The train rolled up to the platform and stopped.

The people inside the subway train were packed in tight. There were no seats, so Kim reached up and grabbed a strap. Kurt held on tight to Kim's leg.

The train started off with a jerk. All the people swayed from side to side. Kurt could hear the train squeaking and creaking.

Soon, the train slowed down. A voice came over the speaker, "This is Clark Street. Next stop is Wall Street."

"Where are we?" Kurt asked Kim.

"This is the last stop in Brooklyn," Kim explained. "Next, the subway crosses over to Manhattan."

"Then can we get off? I'm so squashed I'm having a hard time breathing."

"Hang in there," Kim said. "Some people will get off as soon as we get to Manhattan."

Kim was right. The next stop was Wall Street. Lots of people got off the train.

At last, Kurt and Kim got seats on the train.

"This is much better!" Kurt said.

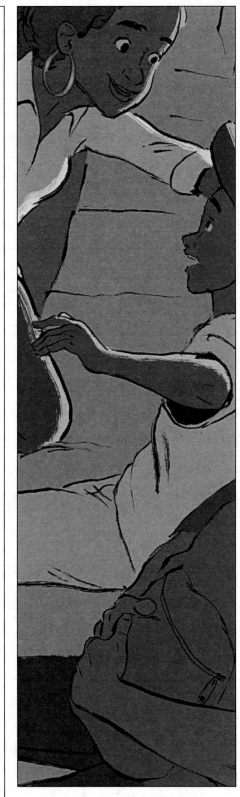

A Snow Day!

Family Member Directions: Have your child read each phrase and then circle the phrases you might see, hear, say, do, or feel on a cold, snowy day.

A cold nose   Bright lights glowing at night

Snowflakes on a window   Snowplows clearing the roads

A rainbow   A green fern

A clown downstairs   "Let's sit by the fire burning in a fireplace."

A tow truck towing a car   Boys surfing the waves

Flying pink birds   Gold coins

Make a snowman   A rabbit hiding

Three blind mice   A hurt tiger

A butterfly   Cold feet

A zebra running down the road   A winter jacket

A frozen lake   Clouds and snow

Blowing snow   A boy swimming

Part I:

1. miss tucker took our class to the fair the fair was on saturday,

    may 2, 2013

2. beth's dad, mr bonner, went with us the fair was on main street

    we went to eat at burger barn after the fair mrs harper made

    cupcakes for our lunch

Part II:

1. mr bob parker   _____

2. mrs jane jones   _____

3. ms tammy binns   _____

4. miss becky willis   _____

Directions: Part I: Have students read and edit the sentences. Part II: Have students rewrite the names correctly.

1. kurt plays goalie for his soccer team, the tigers, on fridays

    _____

    _____

    _____

2. in may jan runs track with her team, the roadrunners, which is coached by mrs turner

    _____

    _____

    _____

3. fran played at bill's house on saturday morning

    _____

    _____

    _____

Directions: Part III: Have students rewrite the sentences correctly. Draw a circle around the common nouns, a box around the proper nouns, and a wiggly line under the verb.

Persuasive Writing Plan

Kind of persuasive writing: _____ Letter _____

1. Opening Sentence:

   _____

   _____

   _____

2. Reason:

   _____

   _____

   _____

3. Reason:

   _____

   _____

   _____

Directions: Have students use this template to plan a persuasive letter.

4.   Reason:

_____

_____

_____

5.   Closing Sentence:

_____

_____

_____

_____

_____

_____

Dear _____,

_____

_____

_____

_____

_____

_____

_____

_____

Sincerely,

_____

Directions: Have students use this template to draft a persuasive letter.

Editing Checklist
for Friendly Letter

Fill out this chart as you edit the draft.

1. Do I have a heading?	
2. Do I have a greeting?	
3. Do I have a body?	
4. Do I have a closing?	
5. Have I added my signature at the end?	
6. Do all of my sentences start with uppercase letters?	
7. Do all of my sentences end with a final mark? (. ? or !)	
8. Have I spelled all of my words correctly?	

Wall Street

At the Wall Street stop a man got on the train. He had on black pants, a black jacket, a crisp white shirt, and a red necktie. He was holding a black case. He looked sharp.

Kurt jabbed Kim with his elbow and whispered, "What do you think his job is? Do you think he is a spy or a secret agent?"

"I don't know," Kim said. "He might be a banker who has a job in a bank on Wall Street."

"What's a bank?"

"A bank is a place where you can keep your cash so it is safe. The bank keeps your cash until you need it and they pay you a bit for saving your cash with them. Since not everyone needs their cash at the same time, the bank has extra cash that they can use to make loans to people who need cash."

"What's a loan?"

"When you get a loan from a bank, the bank lets you borrow some of the cash that it has, and you make a deal to pay the cash back later, plus some fees that the bank adds in."

"You mean you have to pay back more cash than the cash you borrow?"

"That's right."

"Why not just use the cash you've got?" Kurt asked.

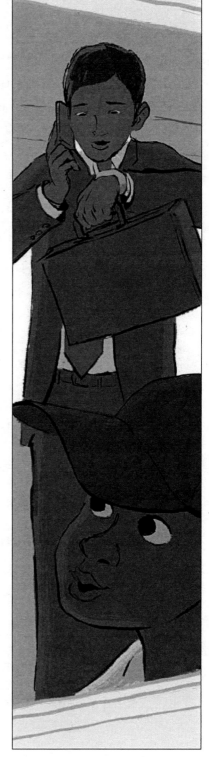

"Well, if you have a lot of cash, you might not need to get a loan. But let's say you plan to open your own store. You would need a lot of cash before you even opened the store! You might not have all of this cash on your own, so you might need a loan to get started."

Kurt dreamed of a store he might like to open and of a banker handing him a big bag of cash. Then he dreamed that he might even like to be a banker himself.

"Do bankers get paid a lot?" Kurt asked.

"Some of them do."

"So why don't you get a job at a bank?"

"Most banks won't hire you unless you have finished two or three years of college. I have just finished one year."

"So it's a hard job to get?"

Kim nodded.

Family Member Directions: Ask your child to mark the circle by the best answer to each question.

1. How did the man who got on the train look?

    ○   The man looked like a mess.

    ○   The man looked sharp.

    ○   The man was singing.

2. What is a bank?

    ○   A bank is a place where you get free food.

    ○   A bank is a place where you take your food to keep it safe.

    ○   A bank is a place where you take your cash to keep it safe.

3. What is a loan?

    ○   A loan is cash that you have to pay back.

    ○   A loan is free cash that you don't have to pay back.

    ○   A loan is a free car that you get to pick out.

4. What is one reason that you would need a loan?

    ○   You might need a loan because you have too much cash.

    ○   You might need a loan because you want to open your own shop.

    ○   You might need a loan because you want to sing a song.

5. Why can't Kim get a job at a bank?

     ○   Kim doesn't want a job at a bank.

     ○   Kim doesn't have sharp clothes.

     ○   Kim hasn't completed two or three years of college.

More Verbs

am	is	are

Directions: Part I: Have students fill in blanks with a form of the verb to be. (am, is, are) Part II: Have students read the sentences and draw a wiggly line under the verb to be in each sentence.

Part I:

1.   I _____ you _____ he _____.

2.   she _____ we _____ they _____.

Part II:

1.   I am at home today.

2.   They are mad.

3.   He is a good athlete.

4.   We are fast runners.

5.   You are my best pal.

6.   She is fun to play with.

7.   You are a girl.

8.   I am from the United States.

Part III:

am	is	are

1. She _____ a good runner.

2. They _____ members of my soccer team.

3. We _____ good readers.

4. I _____ the class helper today.

5. You _____ in the right line.

6. He _____ glad to be in our class.

Part IV:

1. am _____

   _____

2. is _____

   _____

3. are _____

   _____

Persuasive Writing Plan

Kind of persuasive writing: _____ Letter _____

1. Opening Sentence:

   _____

   _____

   _____

2. Reason:

   _____

   _____

   _____

3. Reason:

   _____

   _____

   _____

Directions: Have students use this template to plan a persuasive letter.

Unit 4   83
© 2013 Core Knowledge Foundation

4.   Reason:

_____

_____

_____

5.   Closing Sentence:

_____

_____

_____

Name _____

_____

_____

_____

Dear _____,

_____

_____

_____

_____

_____

_____

_____

_____

Sincerely,

_____

Directions: Have students use this template to draft a persuasive letter.

Editing Checklist
for Persuasive Letter

Fill out this chart as you edit the draft.

1. Do I have a heading?	
2. Do I have a greeting?	
3. Do I have a body?	
4. Do I have a closing?	
5. Have I added my signature at the end?	
6. Do all of my sentences start with uppercase letters?	
7. Do all of my sentences end with a final mark? (. ? or !)	
8. Have I spelled all of my words correctly?	

Spelling Test

1. _____   9. _____

2. _____   10. _____

3. _____   11. _____

4. _____   12. _____

5. _____   13. _____

6. _____   14. _____

7. _____   15. _____

8. _____

Describe the plot of this story in four or five sentences.

_____

_____

_____

_____

_____

_____

_____

_____

_____

_____

Dear Family Member,

The spelling words this week review the four different ways we have learned to spell the sound /ee/ ('e_e' as in *Pete*; 'ee' as in *creek*; 'e' as in *he*; 'ea' as in *meal*).

If at all possible, review the words each evening with your child. You may also suggest your child review the words independently by asking your child to write the words a few times every evening. You will be surprised how much your child can learn in just 10–15 minutes of practice each night.

Continue to have your child read every night. At this point in the year, your child may be ready to begin reading silently. As children start to read silently, they often subvocalize or "whisper read" to themselves. As your child continues to practice reading, he or she may start just moving their lips with no sound; with more practice, he or she will finally feel comfortable reading silently. You can suggest that your child alternate reading a page of a story aloud to you with reading a page silently to himself/herself to encourage the development of silent reading. However, let your child choose whatever way he or she feels most at ease in reading.

'e_e'	'ee'	'e'	'ea'
eve	creek	she	seal
complete	week	we	meal
	meeting	zero	wheat
		fever	squeak
		pretend	

Tricky Word: people

Circle the spellings for each sound.

/ee/	/i/	/ie/
treat	gym	stripe
even	hint	wild
Pete	amethyst	night
centipede	kissed	pie
meter	Brooklyn	cry
wheat	myth	find
complete	bitter	try
repeat	system	sigh
relax	skip	shine
steep	hiccup	tie

This chart shows spellings for the /ie/ sound. Use the chart to fill in Worksheet 16.4.

	'i_e'	'i'	'y'	'ie'	'igh'
b	bike	biker			bright
c	campfire	child	cry	cries	
d	drive	diet driver	dry	dried	
e	excite	excited			
f		find	fly		
g		gigantic			
h	hike	hiking			high
k	kite	kind			
l	life				light
m		mind			might
n	nine	ninth			night
o		Ohio			
p	pride				
q	quite	quiet			
r	rise				right
s	shine slime smile	shining silent smiling spider	satisfy shy sky spy supply	spies	
t	time tired	tiger	try	tried	
w	write	wild writing	Wyoming		

Use the chart on Worksheet 16.3 to fill in the blanks.

1. Count the words on the chart that have the sound /ie/ spelled 'i_e' and write the number here.

    _____

2. Count the words on the chart that have the sound /ie/ spelled 'i' and write the number here.

    _____

3. Count the words on the chart that have the sound /ie/ spelled 'y' and write the number here.

    _____

4. Count the words on the chart that have the sound /ie/ spelled 'ie' and write the number here.

    _____

5. Count the words on the chart that have the sound /ie/ spelled 'igh' and write the number here.

    _____

6. Which spelling for /ie/ has the most words?

    _____

7. Where does the spelling 'igh' tend to be found in a word—at the beginning, in the center, or at the end?

    _____

8. Where does the spelling 'y' as /ie/ tend to be found in a word—at the beginning, in the center, or at the end?

    _____

9. Which words on the chart are proper nouns?

    _____

10. Which word on the chart is an antonym of low?

    _____

11. There are two bugs on the chart. What are they?

    _____

12. Which word on the chart names something that a lot of kids like to ride?

    _____

13. Which word on the chart is a synonym of nice?

    _____

14. Which word on the chart is a synonym of huge?

    _____

15. There is one compound word on the chart. What is it?

    _____

16. Write a sentence that has some words from the chart. Use a lot of words from the chart if you can!

    _____

    _____

Let's Do the Bunny Hop!

Here's How to Play:

1. Assist your child in cutting out the cards on Worksheet 16.7.

2. Shuffle the cards and lay them face down.

3. Each person should write his/her name on one of the bunny hop paths.

4. Draw a card. Read the word on the card. Write the word on the correct space on the bunny path.

5. Put the card back on the bottom of the stack.

6. First person to fill up the bunny path wins!

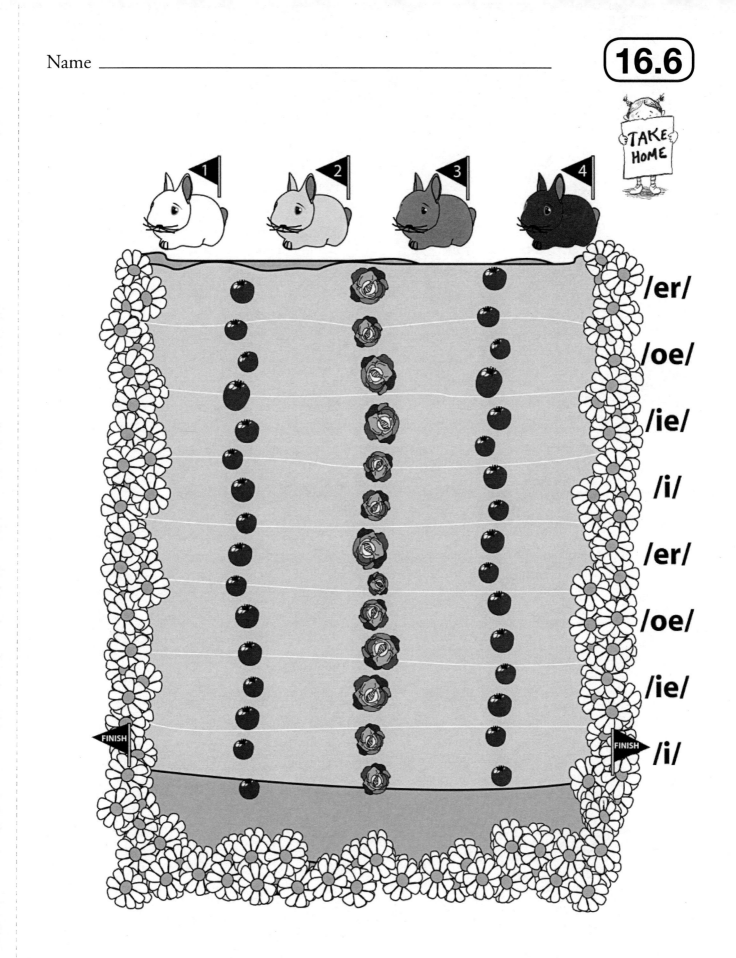

/er/

/oe/

/ie/

/i/

/er/

/oe/

/ie/

/i/

Bunny Hop Cards

servant	find	curb	gym	post	multiply
stirrup	dryer	gold	spider	fellow	nearby
pattern	supply	surrender	silent	elbow	mold
system	old	bright	tiger	owners	disturb
cymbal	cold	swirl	dryer	toll	snow
symbol	below	squirrel	cry	high	blow
bind	yellow	disturb	fry	lies	show
blind	window	myth	most	oxygen	third

Fill in the Blank

Write the best word from the box on the line to finish each sentence.

key	bunny	story	city	baby	shy
myth	chimney	yard	funny	study	donkey

1. A _____ looks a lot like a horse.

2. The grass in the back _____ needs to be mowed.

3. The _____ was crying because he was hungry.

4. Kurt asked his sister to read him a silly _____.

5. Do you have your house _____ so you can unlock the door?

6. I saw a fluffy, white _____ burrow into its hole.

7. There was smoke blowing from the _____ because we had a fire in the fireplace.

8. The Greek _____ we are reading is about gods and goddesses.

Fill in the Blank

Write the best word from the box on the line to finish each sentence.

key	bunny	story	city	baby	shy
myth	chimney	yard	funny	study	donkey

9. What a _____ joke!

10. Don't forget to _____ your spelling words for the test on Friday!

11. Jenny is _____ with people that she does not know well.

12. I do not like the noise of the traffic in the _____.

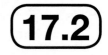

With your partner, make a list of all the foods Kurt has eaten so far during the job hunt.

_____

_____

_____

_____

_____

_____

_____

_____

_____

_____

nurse	easy	light	butterfly	twenty
squirrel	furry	really	angry	body

1. I stayed outside all day and got a sunburn over my entire

   _____.

2. The _____ told me I had a fever.

3. My sister is _____ years old.

4. Math is an _____ subject for me.

5. The _____ ate the corn from the feeder.

6. I did not eat lunch, so I am _____ hungry!

7. Can you turn on the _____?

8. A soft, _____ bunny hopped past the lawn.

9. My mom was _____ when she saw the hole in my
   pants.

10. The _____ flitted from flower to flower.

Family Member Directions: Have your child write the best word from the box to complete each sentence.

yellow	tricky	butterfly	baby	gym	antonym
story	dry	study	supply	crazy	fairy

Directions: Have students write each word in the correct sound box.

'y' > /y/ (yarn)	'y' > /ie/ (my)
'y' > /i/ (myth)	**'y' > /ee/ (funny)**

Plural Nouns

1. Big _____ have subway trains.
   (city)

2. We went to a lot of _____.
   (party)

3. There are six _____!
   (puppy)

4. We picked a bucket of _____.
   (cherry)

5. Cindy likes to hear _____ about elves
   (story)
   and _____.
   (fairy)

Verbs

6. He _____ for his test each night.
   (study)

7. The man _____ to his home.
   (hurry)

8. Jane _____ her green peas in the gravy.
   (bury)

9. The squirrel _____ nuts in his cheeks.
   (carry)

10. Mark _____ Jane next week.
    (marry)

The Daydream

The subway train went on past Wall Street, going north.

Kim looked at the Job Opening ads in the paper.

Kurt looked up at the posters that were hanging on the walls of the train. One of them was a poster of two star baseball players. The players seemed to smile down at Kurt, as if to say, "This is the life, man!"

Kurt stared at the poster and daydreamed. He could hear a man speaking. The man was calling out the play-by-play for a baseball game.

"Two out in the ninth inning," the man said. "The home team is down by two runs. So, Mark, it looks like it's all up to Kurt Gunter at this point."

"Well, James," said a different voice, "Kurt Gunter has had such a good year. As you know, the former spaceship pilot and race car driver is leading the team in hits, home runs, and runs batted in. He has hit the ball so well this year that most fans I've spoken with think he's the bee's knees! In fact, I had a caller on my show, Sports Yap, last week who told me he thinks Gunter should make twice what they pay him."

"So Gunter steps up to the plate. Here's the pitch. It's a strike. The fans are mad. They don't like the call. They think it was a ball. But Gunter himself seems not to mind. He steps back into the box. Here's the pitch. Gunter swings."

Smack!

"Look out, Mark! He got a bit of that one! It's a long fly ball to the left. It's going, it's going. It's out of here! Kurt Gunter has hit a home run! Home run by Gunter! We win! We win!"

"James, I'm telling you, that's why Kurt Gunter is a rich man!"

"Gunter is rounding the bases. He tips his hat to the fans. The fans are going wild! They are shouting, 'Kurt! Kurt! Kurt!'"

Just then Kurt looked up. Kim was shaking him and saying, "Kurt, Kurt, Kurt! This is our stop!"

The Daydream

1. What is on the poster that is hanging on the wall of the subway train?

    A. Basketball players are on the poster.

    B. Baseball players are on the poster.

    C. Football players are on the poster.

2. In Kurt's daydream, why is Kurt a rich man?

    A. Kurt is a race car driver.

    B. Kurt is a banker.

    C. Kurt is a baseball player.

3. In Kurt's daydream, who shouts, "Kurt! Kurt! Kurt!"?

    A. Kurt's fans shout it.

    B. Kim shouts it.

    C. Kurt's mom shouts it.

4. In real life, who shouts, "Kurt, Kurt, Kurt!"?

    A. Kurt's fans shout it.

    B. Kim shouts it.

    C. Kurt's mom shouts it.

5. Describe a daydream you have had.

_____

_____

_____

_____

_____

_____

_____

_____

_____

_____

Part I:

was	were

1. Jack _____ at her house last night.

2. They _____ happy to win last night.

3. Mom _____ at my game yesterday.

4. We _____ glad we saw a show last Saturday.

5. I _____ in first grade last year.

6. They _____ yelling at the party last week.

is	am	are

1. She _____ cold without her jacket.

2. We _____ good pals.

3. They _____ in the parking lot.

4. He _____ on the football team.

5. I _____ happy today.

6. You _____ in the right place.

Part II:

1.   We are at the park today.

     Yesterday _____

     _____.

2.   He is at the party today.

     Last week _____

     _____.

Directions: Part II: Have students draw a wiggly line under the present tense of the verb to be. Then have students write the sentence in the past tense. Lastly, have students draw a wiggly line under the past tense to be verbs.

Spelling Test

1. _____ 9. _____

2. _____ 10. _____

3. _____ 11. _____

4. _____ 12. _____

5. _____ 13. _____

6. _____ 14. _____

7. _____ 15. _____

8. _____

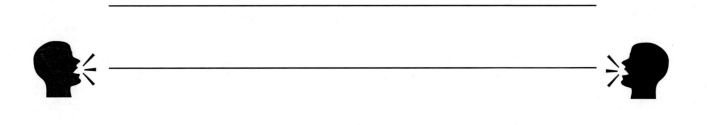

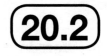
Directions: Part I: Have students draw circles around the common nouns, boxes around the proper nouns, and wiggly lines under the verbs. Part II: Have students make each singular noun into a plural noun. Part III: Have students fill in the bubble beside the correct answer.

Part I:

1.   I was on the subway until Wall Street.

2.   Mr. Fremont is a jolly man.

3.   We were really hungry.

4.   The player hit the baseball out of the park.

5.   Her mom's name is Mrs. Gunter.

Part II:

1 witch, 5 _____   1 child, 2 _____

1 puppy, 2 _____   1 mouse, 3 _____

1 towel, 6 _____   1 firefly, 4 _____

1 squirrel, 9 _____   1 elf, 8 _____

Part III:

1.   ○   ms Ginger Marks   3.   ○   Mrs Lynn west
     ○   Ms Ginger Marks   ○   mrs. lynn west
     ○   Ms. Ginger Marks   ○   Mrs. Lynn West

2.   ○   Mr Jim Burton   4.   ○   miss sheryl parker
     ○   Mr. Jim Burton   ○   Miss Sheryl Parker
     ○   mr. Jim Burton   ○   Miss. Sheryl Parker

1.   is mrs wiggins a teacher at western high

2.   a mouse ran past the door and startled mr smith

3.   my birthday is on monday, march 7th

4.   i am going to eat at the burger king that is on oak street

5.   can you help miss winters find the state of maine on the map

Part V:

am	are	is

1.   He _____ very sleepy.

2.   You _____ a really good pal.

3.   I _____ not really hungry right now.

4.   She _____ smart.

Part VI:

was	were

1.   We _____ at the park.

2.   I _____ so mad yesterday!

3.   They _____ satisfied with their gift.

Directions: Have students edit the letter from Mr. Mowse as individuals, partners, small groups, or as an entire class.

The Mowse Hole

Your Classroom Wall

Mowse Land, U.S.A.

january 15, 2014

Dear Friends,

i wud like to ask u to let me sit wit u when u do your reading skils lessons

i think the lesons sound vere interesting i wud lik to learn how 2 write betr.

I lik 2 write it helps mee think abut things i wud lik 2 reed some uv your story bookz I like the story abut kim and kurt. Do u think i coud git a job

Please ask your teacher if i can come 2 your class i promise 2 b gud and not 2 skare anee1

Sincerely,

mr mowse

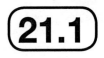

Fill in the Blank

salty	caught	dawn	wallpaper
false	always	almanac	walrus

1. The sun rises in the east at _____.

2. My sister is _____ last to wake up at our house.

3. I went to the store with my mom to pick out _____ to decorate my bedroom walls.

4. The _____ says that the first snowfall this year will be in December.

5. The test will be a true or _____ test.

6. There was a sudden thunderstorm and we got _____ in the rain.

7. I got very thirsty because the peanuts were _____.

8. A _____ has whiskers and long white tusks.

| Billy | daddy | cavity | puppy | dirty |
| daisy | easy | chilly | jelly | candy |

Down

1. baby dog
2. not clean
3. a kind of flower
4. sweet treat
5. toast and _____
7. a boy's name

Side to Side

2. antonym of mommy
4. hole in your tooth
6. not difficult
8. a bit cold

Directions: Use the clues to complete the crossword puzzle.

Name _____

Dear Family Member,

  Please ask your child to read each sentence carefully. In some sentences the word below the blank will fit in the blank as it is. In other sentences, the word will need to be changed into its plural form.

1. I have three _____.
    (cavity)

2. Is the _____ wet?
    (baby)

3. How many _____ does the farmer have?
    (pony)

4. Did you have a _____?
    (penny)

5. Is he in the _____ or navy?
    (army)

6. All of my _____ will be at the party.
    (buddy)

7. How many _____ did you pick?
    (daisy)

8. We all had fat _____.
    (tummy)

9. How many _____ did you eat?
    (cherry)

10. What is your _____?
    (hobby)

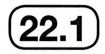

The Tally

1. Who is Mr. Fremont?

    A. Mr. Fremont is a clerk at the store.

    B. Mr. Fremont is the store owner.

    C. Mr. Fremont is a shopper in the store.

2. What did Mr. Fremont ask Kim to do?

    A. He asked her to add up the cost of some food.

    B. He asked her to use the front door.

    C. He asked her to place items on the shelves.

3. Why did Mr. Fremont tell Kim not to use the cash register?

    A. The cash register was broken.

    B. He wanted to see if Kim could add up the cost herself.

    C. He thinks Kim does not know how to use the cash register.

4. How did Kim complete the tally?

    A. She used a calculator to enter the prices.

    B. She checked the prices on the shelves.

    C. She wrote the prices on paper and then added them.

5. How did Mr. Fremont show he was pleased with Kim?

    A. He clapped his hands.

    B. He told Kim that she could have a job at the store.

    C. He told Kim to add the sales tax.

6. Why did Mr. Fremont hand Kim twenty bucks?

    A. He wanted her to place the twenty bucks in the cash register.

    B. He wanted to pay her for taking inventory and doing the tally.

    C. He wanted to help her pay for her subway ride.

7. How did Kim feel at the end of the story?

    A. She was sad she did not get a job.

    B. She was mad after doing the inventory.

    C. She was excited because she found a job.

8. When did Mr. Fremont tell Kim she could start her job?

    A. He told her she could start today.

    B. He told her she could start next week.

    C. He told her she could start next year.

9. If Kim showed up at her job at 9:00 on her first day, she would

    A. be late.

    B. be right on time.

    C. be there at the wrong time.

10. Who did Kim call?

    A. Kim called Kurt.

    B. Kim called Mr. Fremont.

    C. Kim called her mom.

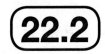
Which is Right?

Directions: Part I: Have students fill in the bubble next to the correct answer. Part II: Have students draw a circle around the common nouns, a box around the proper nouns, and a wiggly line under the verbs. Part III: Have students rewrite the sentence correctly.

Part I

1. ○ Mr Tom White
   ○ Mr. Tom White
   ○ Mr. tom White

2. ○ Ms Pam Foster
   ○ Ms. pam Foster
   ○ Ms. Pam Foster

3. ○ Mrs Jan Hunter
   ○ Mrs jan hunter.
   ○ Mrs. Jan Hunter

4. ○ Miss. Gail Smith
   ○ Miss Gail Smith
   ○ Miss Gail smith

Part II

1. Grasshoppers hop high off the ground. (2 nouns and 1 verb)

2. Sally was really happy last Friday. (2 nouns and 1 verb)

3. I am at home. (1 noun and 1 verb)

Part III

1. i hope we go to oak park on saturday

_____

_____

2. is mr jones invited to the party on march 1, 2011

_____

_____

shelf_____   child _____

dress _____   pen _____

church _____   wife _____

elf _____   box _____

mouse _____   man _____

wish _____   foot _____

Part V

am	are	is

1. He _____ happy at the party today.

2. I _____ in second grade this year.

3. We _____ not going outside today.

4. They _____ having pie for a snack.

5. You _____ always on time.

6. She _____ in her room playing.

Part VI

was	were

1. She _____ happy when she rode the bus yesterday.

2. We _____ all really tired last night.

3. They _____ thrilled to have a party last week.

4. I _____ glad my pal came over yesterday.

5. He _____ my partner in the game last Friday.

6. You _____ the last one to finish the race.

Directions: Part IV: Have students rewrite each word as a plural. Parts V and VI: Have students fill in the blank with the correct word.

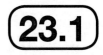

The Visit

Kim was happy that she had found a summer job.

"Let's go and visit Mom," she said. "She will be finished teaching by the time we get there."

Kim held up a hand to hail a cab. A yellow cab screeched to a stop on the side of the street. "Where to?" asked the driver. Kim told him the address.

They made it safely. Kim paid the driver. She and Kurt went in to see their mom. Mrs. Gunter gave Kim a big hug. Kurt snuck in between them so he could be part of the hug, too. Then Kim told her mom how they had spent the day. She told her mom how she had used math to help her get the job at the grocery. By the end of the story, Mrs. Gunter was beaming. "You see," she said. "I told you math would help you out one day."

"I never dreamed I would have a job in a grocery," added Kim, "but I think it's going to be a good job for me."

"It may not be the job of your dreams," said her mom. "But it's a job. If you study hard in college, you will have a chance to get the job of your dreams some day. Until then, just do a good job and save as much of your paycheck as you can."

Mom said, "Let's celebrate Kim's new job by going down to Battery Park for a picnic. Are you two hungry for dinner?"

"You bet!" said Kurt. They went to a sub shop nearby. Mrs. Gunter ordered a sub for each of them, plus some snacks and drinks. Then Mrs. Gunter hailed a cab. The cab took them down the West Side Highway. It dropped them off in Battery Park.

Kim was happy that she had found herself a summer job. 11
"Let's go and visit Mom," she said. "She will be finished 22
teaching by the time we get there." Kim held up a hand 34
to hail a cab. A yellow cab screeched to a stop on the side 48
of the street. "Where to?" asked the driver. Kim told him 59
the address. They made it safely. Kim paid the driver. She 70
and Kurt went in to see their mom. Mrs. Gunter gave Kim 82
a big hug. Kurt snuck in between them so he could be 94
part of the hug, too. Then Kim told her mom how they 106
had spent the day. She told her mom how she had used 118
math to help her get the job at the grocery. By the end of 132
the story, Mrs. Gunter was beaming. "You see," she said. 142
"I told you math would help you out one day." "I never 154
dreamed I would have a job in a grocery," added Kim, "but 166
I think it's going to be a good job for me." "It may not be 181
the job of your dreams," said her mom. "But it's a job. If 194
you study hard in college, you will have a chance to get the 207
job of your dreams some day. Until then, just do a good 219
job and save as much of your paycheck as you can." 230
Mom said, "Let's celebrate Kim's new job by going down 240
to Battery Park for a picnic. Are you two hungry for 251
dinner?" "You bet!" said Kurt. They went to a sub shop 262
nearby. Mrs. Gunter ordered a sub for each of them, 272
plus some snacks and drinks. Then Mrs. Gunter hailed a 282
cab. The cab took them down the West Side Highway. It 293
dropped them off in Battery Park. 299

Name _____

(Insert total words read) _____ – (Errors) = _____ WCPM (Words Correct Per Minute)

Record student's words per minute _____

WCPM divided by Words Read = _____% accuracy

Please place a check mark in front of each question answered correctly.

_____ 1. What is Mrs. Gunter's job? (She is a teacher.)

_____ 2. Where will Kim work for the summer? (Kim will work at a grocery store.)

_____ 3. What skill did Kim use to help her get her job? (Kim used her math skills.)

_____ 4. What 2 things did Mrs. Gunter tell Kim to do at her summer job? (Mrs. Gunter told Kim to do a good job and save as much of her money as she could.)

_____ 5. How did the family celebrate? (The family celebrated with a picnic in the park.)

_____/5 total questions correct

5 questions correct – 100%

4 questions correct – 80%

3 questions correct – 60%

2 questions correct – 40%

1 question correct – 20%

Name _____

Multi-Dimensional Fluency Scale
The Three P's

Circle one score for the student's reading. Comments may be made in the appropriate section.

Descriptions			Circle One	
Phrasing	**Prosody**	**Pace**	Score	Comments
Mostly reads word-by-word	Many long pauses, rereads, and multiple attempts	Very slow and laborious	**Labored**	
Attempts to make text meaningful but still struggles with decoding words	Attempts phrases, may still have word-by-word reading for some of passage	Still hesitant and not fluid; very choppy	**Improving**	
May stumble occasionally over words	May read too fast and/or too slow without regard to textual signals	Generally appropriate expression and rate	**Mostly Fluent**	
Good expression and engagement with text	Observation of functional text signals and meaningful expression	Smooth, appropriate pace for the text	**Fluent**	

Adapted from scale by Zutell & Rasinski, 1991.

(Teacher: You will record this information on the Oral Reading Fluency Assessment Results Chart located in the Teacher Guide in Lesson 23.)

Unit 4 **145**

Directions: Have students circle the word called by the teacher.

1.	fern	first	find	furl
2.	burnt	bend	burn	bunt
3.	fist	first	find	furl
4.	mist	math	miss	myth
5.	find	kite	kin	kind
6.	neat	nice	night	might
7.	spit	spy	sky	sight
8.	sowing	now	snow	sow
9.	ever	ease	even	easy
10.	luck	ducky	lucky	leaky

11. clerk	cent	can't	cart
12. born	burst	barn	fun
13. thirst	thin	thick	then
14. germ	ginger	gym	gap
15. mend	mid	made	mind
16. sight	sitter	singer	sap
17. seal	sky	seek	sail
18. blow	yelling	yells	howl
19. bent	met	see	mending
20. fume	furl	fern	funny

Synonyms

| fix | fib | silent | silly | pony |
| speak | cry | myth | part | shriek |

Directions: Have students use the words from the box to write a synonym on the line next to each word.

1. funny _____

2. legend _____

3. quiet _____

4. lie _____

5. sob _____

6. piece _____

7. horse _____

8. repair _____

9. scream _____

10. talk _____

Antonyms

long	beginning	erase	soggy	quickly
quiet	kind	hard	smooth	dark

1. easy   _____

2. slowly   _____

3. ending   _____

4. brief   _____

5. mean   _____

6. light   _____

7. bumpy   _____

8. loud   _____

9. dry   _____

10. write   _____

Directions: Have students use the words from the box to write an antonym on the line next to each word.

Name _____

Compound Words

body	fly	shirt	light	end
tie	print	mint	life	pool

1. pepper _____

2. under _____

3. finger _____

4. wild _____

5. neck _____

6. butter _____

7. flash _____

8. every _____

9. week _____

10. whirl _____

Directions: Have students add a word from the box to the end of each numbered word to create a compound word. Write the new compound word on the line.

Unit 4 **151**

Nouns

Directions: Have students circle the nouns in the sentences. The number of nouns in a sentence is written at the end of the sentence.

Wear your yellow skirt. (1)

1. Kitties and puppies are cute. (2)

2. The pie has blackberries and cherries. (3)

3. The pond reflected the moonlight. (2)

4. The athlete is holding a football. (2)

5. These lyrics are really good! (1)

6. The spy is hiding behind the trees. (2)

7. Venus is a planet. (2)

Mixed Plural Nouns

cow _____   chip _____

girl _____   foot _____

tooth _____   wish _____

desk _____   goose _____

mouse _____   child _____

1. mice _____

2. man _____

3. men _____

4. geese _____

5. teeth _____

6. children _____

7. foot _____

8. child _____

9. tooth _____

Irregular Plural Nouns

wolf	leaves	loaf	loaves
elf	wolves	leaf	scarf
half	scarves	halves	elves

1. Many _____ fell from the trees.

2. Santa has many _____.

3. I saw a bright red _____ from a tree on the ground.

4. Mrs. Barton baked three _____, one for each of my teachers.

5. Mom has a new green _____ to wear.

6. We cut the paper into two _____.

7. Can you give me _____ of your muffin?

8. There can be _____ in the woods.

Directions: Have students select the word from the box that best fits the sentence.

wolf	leaves	loaf	loaves
elf	wolves	leaf	scarf
half	scarves	halves	elves

9. There was only one _____ left on the store shelf.

10. There is a big, bad _____ in the tale "The Three Little Pigs."

11. There were nice _____ at the store.

12. In the magic tale, an _____ found gold at the end of the rainbow.

Titles and Proper Nouns

Directions: Part I: Have students write the titles correctly. Part II: Have students write the sentences correctly.

Part I:

1. ms tyler   _____

2. miss smith   _____

3. mr winters   _____

4. mrs landers   _____

Part II:

1. mom baked a cake for mr woods on saturday

    _____

    _____

    _____

2. can miss rogers help us with our meeting in september

    _____

    _____

    _____

3. it is fun to go to burns park on main street each friday

    _____

    _____

    _____

4. mr parker will be our teacher this thursday at parks school

_____

_____

_____

5. is mrs green's house on spring street or main street

_____

_____

_____

More Titles, Proper Nouns, and Verbs

Directions: Part I: Have students fill in the bubble next to the one written correctly. Part II: Circle the nouns and draw a wiggly line under the verb in each sentence.

Part I:

1. ○ ms gail butler
   ○ Ms Gail Butler
   ○ Ms. Gail Butler

2. ○ Mrs Jane ball
   ○ mrs. jane ball
   ○ Mrs. Jane Ball

3. ○ mr jeff tucker
   ○ Mr Jeff Tucker
   ○ Mr. Jeff Tucker

4. ○ miss beth parker
   ○ Miss. Beth Parker
   ○ Miss Beth Parker

Part II:

1. The leaves fall from the trees in the fall. (3 nouns and 1 verb)

2. The children played outside all day. (2 nouns and 1 verb)

3. Horses eat hay and oats each day. (4 nouns and 1 verb)

4. The man ran after the cart. (2 nouns and 1 verb)

5. The teacher plays with the children. (2 nouns and 1 verb)

6. Write your own sentence using nouns and verbs:

_____

_____

_____

Verbs

Part I:

run	runs

1. I   _____

2. You   _____

3. He   _____

4. She   _____

5. It   _____

6. We   _____

7. They   _____

Part II:

am	is	are

1. I   _____

2. You   _____

3. He   _____

am	is	are

4. She _____

5. It _____

6. We _____

7. They _____

Part III:

1. am_____

_____

_____

2. is_____

_____

_____

3. are_____

_____

_____

Directions: Part III: Have students write three sentences using am, is, and are.

Present Tense *to be*

Example: I am running.

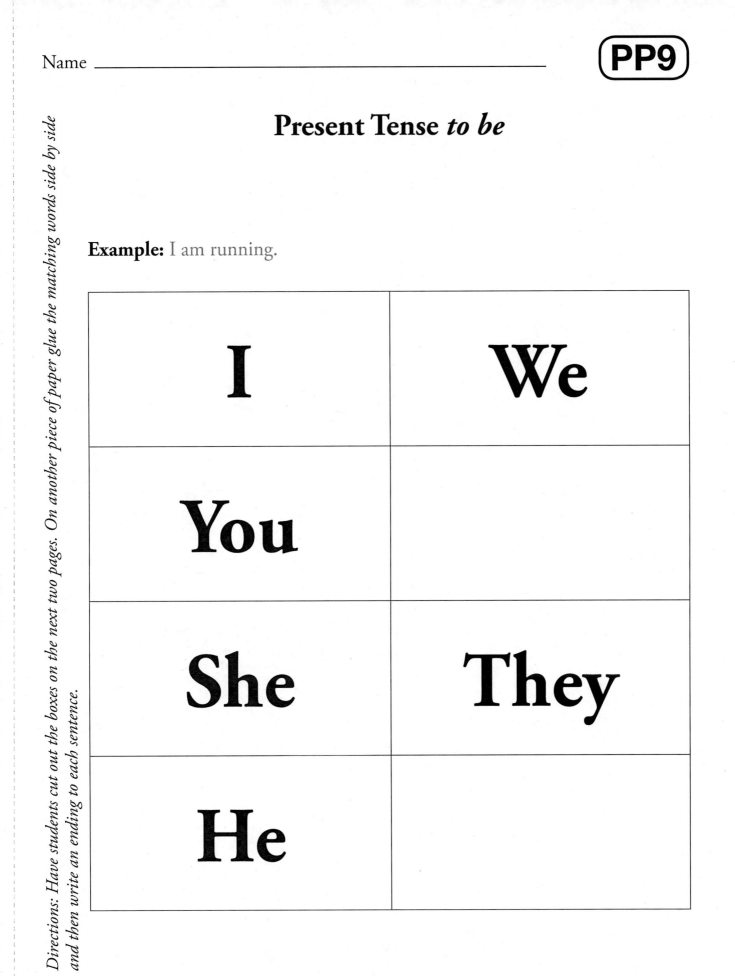

I	We
You	
She	They
He	

are	**is**
are	**is**
are	**am**

Directions: Have students cut out the boxes on this page. On another piece of paper glue the matching words side by side and then write an ending to each sentence.

Past Tense *to be*

Fill in each blank with *was* or *were*.

1. I _____

2. You _____

3. She _____

4. We _____

5. They _____

6. It _____

7. He _____

Write two sentences using the word *was*.

1. _____

   _____

   _____

2. _____

   _____

   _____

Write two sentences using the word *were*.

1. _____

   _____

   _____

2. _____

   _____

   _____

Spelling Worksheets Lessons 1–5

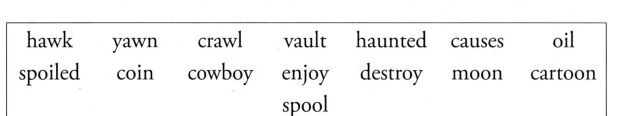

hawk	yawn	crawl	vault	haunted	causes	oil
spoiled	coin	cowboy	enjoy	destroy	moon	cartoon
		spool				

Use the words in the word box to complete the puzzle.

Down

1.   The sun, the _____, and the stars are in the sky.

3.   You do this when you are sleepy.

4.   You might be this if you always get your way.

5.   What _____ a cold?

7.   I would _____ some ice cream.

8.   A word for jump

9.   A comic strip

11. You fry food in this.

Side to Side

2.   He rides the plains with cows.

5.   A penny or a dime

6.   Large bird that eats chickens

9.   A baby will do this before walking.

10. Do not _____ my vase.

12. A _____ of kite string

14. A house might be _____ if there are ghosts.

Spelling Worksheets Lessons 6–10

Use the words in the word box to complete the puzzle.

car	bar	store	chore	nerve	serve	stir
girl	bird	fur	hurt	turn	purse	all
			shirt			

Down

1. I _____ my knee when I fell.

3. Your mom might say you are getting on her last _____.

4. A job you do at home

5. You go here to get milk.

6. My cat is shedding her _____.

8. I have a stain on my _____.

9. Not a boy but a _____

11. I added a _____ to the fence.

Side to Side

2. Can you _____ on the light?

4. You ride in this.

5. A waiter will _____ you dinner.

7. My mom has a big _____.

10. A crow is one of these.

12. Can _____ of us go with you?

13. Please _____ the cake batter.

Spelling Worksheets Lessons 11–15

Use the words in the word box to complete the puzzle.

elbow	yellow	below	rainbow	snow	sorrow	arrow
plow	flowers	your	powder	shower	meow	chow
			growling			

Down

2. to eat

3. You might take this to get clean.

6. many colors in an arch in the sky

7. a sound a dog might make

9. the bend of your arm

12. You might put this on a baby.

13. A farmer might do this to the soil.

15. A cat makes this sound.

Side to Side

1. This is _____ scarf.

4. sadness

5. plants that bloom

8. not on top

10. White flakes that fall from the sky in winter.

11. bow and _____

14. A buttercup flower is this color.

Spelling Worksheets Lessons 16–20

Use the words in the word box to complete the puzzle.

eve	creek	week	meeting	she	we	fever
zero	pretend	squeak	meal	wheat	seal	people
		complete				

Down

2.   seven days long

3.   I saw a _____ swimming at the zoo.

5.   I will see you at the _____.

7.   There were lots of _____ in the crowd.

9.   the night before

10.   to finish

12.   He is not going, so _____ is not going.

Side to Side

1.   Dinner is a ____.

3.   A toy for dogs might make this sound.

4.   smaller than a river

6.   Flour is made from this grain.

7.   not real

8.   If you are sick, you may have a _____.

11.   a number less than 1

13.   _____ are happy!

'er', 'ir', 'ur' as /er/

Choose the best word from the box to complete each sentence.

hurt	circus	skirts
burned	birthday	birds
surprise	Saturday	clerks
thirsty	dirty	

1. I like pants better than _____.

2. Be careful near the edge! I don't want you to get
    _____.

3. Is the party on Friday or _____?

4. In the nest sat three baby _____.

5. Shirley saw clowns at the _____.

6. Is the party a _____?

7. Abby got lots of gifts for her _____.

8. Can I have something to drink? I am so _____.

9. My mom makes me shower when I am _____.

'er', 'ir', 'ur' as /er/

Choose the best word from the box to fill in each sentence.

hurt	circus	skirts
burned	birthday	birds
surprise	Saturday	clerks
thirsty	dirty	

10. The fire _____ all night.

11. The store _____ were very helpful.

Fill in _yes_ or _no_ on each blank.

1.   Can a bird swim in a birdbath? _____

2.   Is today Thursday? _____

3.   Do fish have fur? _____

4.   Can tigers run fast? _____

5.   Does a dime have corners? _____

6.   Is a goose a bird? _____

7.   Does a nurse use a thermometer? _____

8.   Does a shepherd take care of squirrels? _____

9.   Is Saturn a planet? _____

10. Do you have to go to class on Saturday? _____

1. The _____ will make a nest in the spring.
   (bard   bird)

2. Her hair has lots of _____.
   (church   curls)

3. My mom's _____ has lots of stuff in it.
   (nurse   purse)

4. Can you ask that _____ to skip rope with me?
   (grill   girl)

5. The _____ gave me a shot in the arm.
   (purse   nurse)

6. If you can ride the waves in the sea, then you
   can _____.
   (sure   surf)

7. Last year I was in _____ grade.
   (fist   first)

8. I like the _____ ice cream cones at the shop.
   (swirl   sell)

9. To make butter, you have to _____ cream.
   (churn   curl)

10. My _____ is green and red for the holidays.
    (skirt   skit)

11. Dad lets me _____ the pancake batter on Saturday
    (skirt   stir)
    mornings.

12. The cat's _____ is so soft.
    (fur   first)

Directions: Have students write the best word to complete each sentence.

Part I:

curly	lever	thirty
baker	maker	mother
hurry	birch	western
turning	thirsty	person
dirty	interest	sunburn
bird	squirrel	hurt
curb	faster	over

Part II:

circus	serve	harm	whirl
turn	fork	purr	pattern
fur	cold	bird	nerve
curb	dare	further	dirt
perch	lever	first	best
surrender	starve	stirrup	sir
bird	arch	perfect	disturb

Directions: Part I: Have students circle the spelling in each word that stands for the /er/ sound. Part II: Have students cross out the word in each row that DOES NOT contain the /er/ sound.

Sound Sorting

kick	gym	gift	hill	myth	lip
syllable	milk	antonym	synonym	acting	did

Directions: Have students read the words in the box aloud. Then have students circle the letter for the /i/ sound in each word. Then write the words with the /i/ sound spelled 'i' under skin and the words with the /i/ sound spelled 'y' under system.

'i' like *skin*

kick

_____

_____

_____

_____

_____

_____

_____

'y' like *system*

_____

_____

_____

_____

_____

_____

_____

Last Friday, Mike and his dad visited the wildlife park

in Ohio. Mike was most excited to see the tigers, but as

soon as he spied them, he became frightened. (Mike is just

five.) His dad tried to quiet him, but Mike started crying

and would not stop. He was terrified of the tigers! At last,

Mike's dad asked Mike if he'd like to see the pythons. Mike

nodded and his sobs subsided. He was quiet as he and his

dad tried to find the pythons, but once they found them,

Mike started smiling and chatting up a storm.

Directions: Have students circle all of the spellings for the /i/ sound.

Use the words from the word box to fill in the puzzle.

light	might	night	right	high

Down

1. I _____ like an ice pop.

2. We can see the stars at _____.

4. Put the book on the _____ shelf.

Side to Side

3. Turn _____ at the corner.

5. Please turn on the _____.

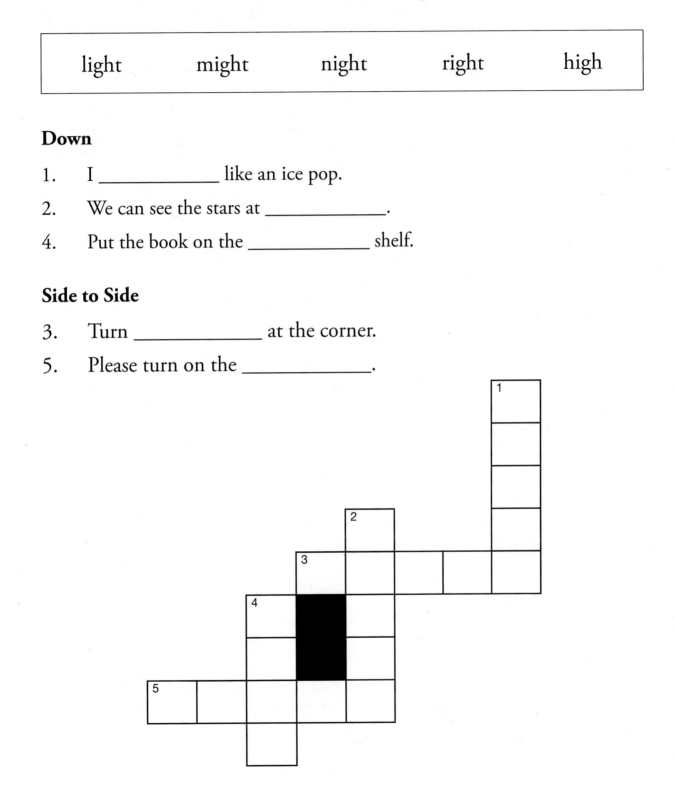

Directions: If the word on the star has the /ie/ sound, color it blue. If the word on the star has the /y/ sound, color it yellow.

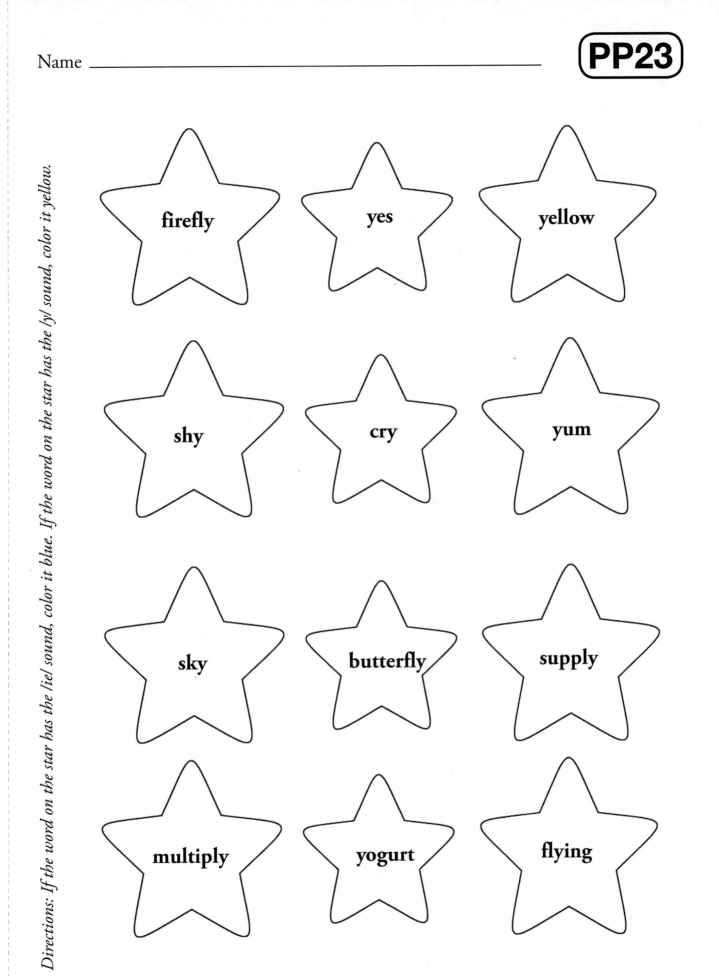

firefly

yes

yellow

shy

cry

yum

sky

butterfly

supply

multiply

yogurt

flying

Fill in the Blank

Directions: Have students read the words in the box aloud. Have students write the best word from the box to complete each sentence.

cold	yodel	scold	solo	cola
mold	hold	banjo	moment	open

1. Will you _____ the door?

2. A _____ is a kind of shout or call.

3. Please wait one _____ and then we will all go to the store.

4. To sing by yourself means to sing a _____.

5. Would you like a _____ to drink?

6. There was green _____ on my sandwich, so I didn't eat it.

7. Can you _____ my mittens?

8. My mom might _____ me if I am not home on time.

9. My sister can play the _____.

10. I am so _____, I think I will just freeze.

This morning, my mom gave me a yell<u>ow</u> pot filled with br<u>ow</u>n soil. She told me that the soil had a fl<u>ow</u>er seed in it. I set the pot on my wind<u>ow</u>sill and waited, but the flower did not gr<u>ow</u>. I put the pot in the sh<u>ow</u>er to water the seed, but the flower did not grow. I placed the pot where the sun would shine on it, but the flower did not grow. I placed the pot in a shad<u>ow</u>, but the flower still did not grow. I fr<u>ow</u>ned and was just about to thr<u>ow</u> it out. At last, my mom said to me, "Don't you kn<u>ow</u> that flowers grow slowly?" Well, n<u>ow</u> I kn<u>ow</u>!

/oe/ like *snow*	/ou/ like *cow*
_____	_____
_____	_____
_____	_____
_____	_____
_____	_____
_____	_____
_____	_____
_____	_____

© 2013 Core Knowledge Foundation

Fill in the blank with *yes* or *no*.

1. Can flowers frown? _____

2. Have you ever seen a show? _____

3. Is clam chowder something to eat? _____

4. Are you a snowman? _____

5. Can a man blow a horn in a car? _____

6. Is your elbow part of your arm? _____

7. Do you use a towel to dry off after a shower? _____

8. Can you look out a window? _____

9. Can a cow bow? _____

10. Can a pig grow wings? _____

11. Is the grass yellow? _____

12. Can a firefly glow at night? _____

13. Is *up* the antonym of *down*? _____

14. Can a spider growl? _____

15. Do you like clowns? _____

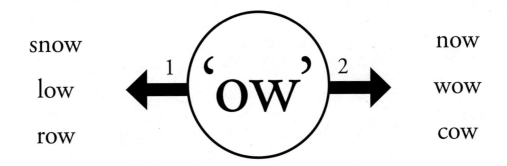

	/oe/ like *snow*	/ou/ like *now*
The king is wearing a <u>crown</u>.		crown
That boy needs to take a <u>shower</u>.		
Troy has some food in his <u>bowl</u>.		
The baby pool is very <u>shallow</u>.		
On Hugo's bed, there are two <u>pillows</u>.		
The starving tiger <u>growled</u>.		
Jake looked at the sky and saw a <u>rainbow</u>.		

If a square has a word with the spelling 'ow' sounded /oe/, make it yellow. If a square has a word with the spelling 'ow' sounded /ou/, make it brown.

crown	now	know	owl	own
show	grow	power	follow	below
crowded	slowly	window	town	snow
yellow	drown	narrow	flow	brown
cow	throw	flower	blow	bowl

If a square has a word with the spelling 'e' sounded /ee/, make it green. If a square has a word with the spelling 'e' sounded /e/, make it yellow.

seven	them	then	being	western
below	get	result	went	maybe
because	never	decide	men	require
best	tell	reply	next	seed
end	bellow	zero	better	destroy

Use the words from the word box to fill in the puzzle.

lady	baby	crazy	gravy	tasty
shaky	tummy	bunny	sunny	wavy

Down

1. I get _____ when I am cold.

2. My hair is curly and _____.

4. I like _____ and rolls.

6. _____ and the Tramp is the name of a film.

8. It is a hot and _____ day.

Side to Side

3. Ice cream is _____.

5. Are you _____?

7. A _____ can crawl.

9. My _____ is filled with good food.

Katie and Molly and their mom took a cab from their hotel to the beach. At the beach, all three smeared sunblock all over their skin. It was hot so they got in the sea for a bit. Then they looked for seashells. After that, Katie and Molly played volleyball with some teenagers. Katie made some really sweet plays. (She's quite the athlete.) In fact, a small group formed to look at her play. After the game, Katie and Molly and their mom started to feel like they could use some food. They left the beach to find something to eat. What a good day!

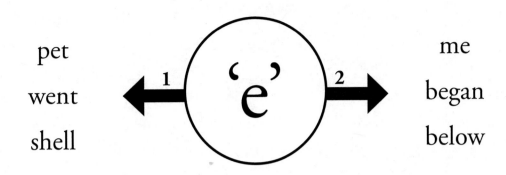

pet

went

shell

me

began

below

	/e/ like *pet*	/ee/ like *me*
I find sweets hard to r<u>e</u>sist.		resist
Should w<u>e</u> go east or west?		
The horse jumped the f<u>e</u>nce.		
I saw a cow at the rod<u>e</u>o.		
If you make a mistake, <u>e</u>rase it.		
Who came in s<u>e</u>cond place?		
Is it on the right or the l<u>e</u>ft?		
Batman is my h<u>e</u>ro.		
I will write a r<u>e</u>port for homework.		

Directions: Have students write the words with the tricky spelling 'e' sounded /e/ under pet and the words with the tricky spelling 'e' sounded /ee/ under me.

Sound Sorting

fever	bench	behind
zebra	maybe	tense
eleven	went	seven

/e/ like *pet*	/ee/ like *me*
	fever

Directions: Have students write the words with the tricky spelling 'e' sounded /e/ under pet and the words with the tricky spelling 'e' sounded /ee/ under me.

myth   try
system   by
cylinder   fly

funny   yes
fifty   yet
sandy   yuck

'y'

2   3   1   4

	funny	*myth*	*try*	*yes*
The grass in our yard is green.				
We watched the Olympics on TV.				
We are visiting Brooklyn this week.				
Do not swat that fly!				
I have not seen her in a year.				
A baby cat is called a kitty.				
She is soft-spoken and shy.				

Directions: Have students write the words with the tricky spelling 'y' sounded /i/ under myth, the words with the tricky spelling 'y' sounded /ee/ under funny, the words with the tricky spelling 'y' sounded /ie/ under try, and the words with the tricky spelling 'y' sounded /y/ under yes.

Sound Sorting

empty	very	satisfy	system
yawn	energy	really	multiply
story	gym	study	yuck

funny   **myth**   **try**   **yes**

© 2013 Core Knowledge Foundation

Directions: Have students write the words with the tricky spelling 'y' sounded /ee/ under funny, the words with the tricky spelling 'y' sounded /i/ under myth, the words with the tricky spelling 'y' sounded /ie/ under try, and the words with the tricky spelling 'y' sounded /y/ under yes.

If a square has a word with the letter 'y' sounded /ee/, make it green. If a square has a word with the letter 'y' sounded /i/, make it yellow. If a square has a word with the letter 'y' sounded /ie/, make it red. If a square has a word with the letter 'y' sounded /y/, make it brown.

try	system	year	dry	simply
gym	sky	likely	plenty	funny
yet	gingerly	Brooklyn	yes	supply
flying	beyond	myth	easy	copy
happy	daddy	satisfy	lynx	yelled

Mixed Practice

Fill in the blank with *yes* or *no*

1. Do ducks have feet? _____

2. Is a synonym the same as an antonym? _____

3. Is a spider bigger than a tiger? _____

4. Are pies made with a cherry filling? _____

5. Can a butterfly cry? _____

6. Do ponies frighten you? _____

7. Is a centipede a person? _____

8. Are you ten years old? _____

9. Can flies speak? _____

10. Is a baby lighter than a house? _____

11. Is surfing a sport? _____

12. Is a pie the same as a cake? _____

13. Can you drink cookies? _____

14. Can a key unlock a house? _____

15. Do you play the horn? _____

16. Can a spider drive a car? _____

17. Can a pony fly? _____

18. Does a necktie go on your leg? _____

19. Is a hippo light? _____

20. Can a pig read a book? _____

Mixed Practice

toads croak	goats eat
gray seal	wren nest
ringing bell	birds fly
running donkey	tiger growls
groaning mule	coast waves
mound of dirt	beaver cheek
steam dryer	pig squeal
mean well	sleek cat
goat herd	black coal
tiger's den	bird nest

swell time	crawling snake
robe of gold	red fox
wet nose	slow goat
fur coat	fast horse
queen's crown	sheep bleating
dog chow	broken rope
raccoon mask	wise owl
lean steel	soccer coach
fell swoop	spelling bee
hen's pen	splash artist
flying dove	math whiz

Tricky 'y'

Add 's' or 'es' to each of the following words. Be careful! Don't get tricked! Sometimes you need to change the 'y' to 'i' and sometimes you don't!

1. play   _____

2. try   _____

3. tray   _____

4. fly   _____

5. pay   _____

6. hurry   _____

7. joy   _____

8. study   _____

9. puppy   _____

10. toy   _____

11. kitty   _____

12. enjoy   _____

13. story   _____

14. boy   _____

15. butterfly   _____

16. day   _____

17. dragonfly   _____

18. lady   _____

Add 's' or 'es' to each word. Don't fall down the steps by changing a 'y' to 'i' when you don't need to do so!

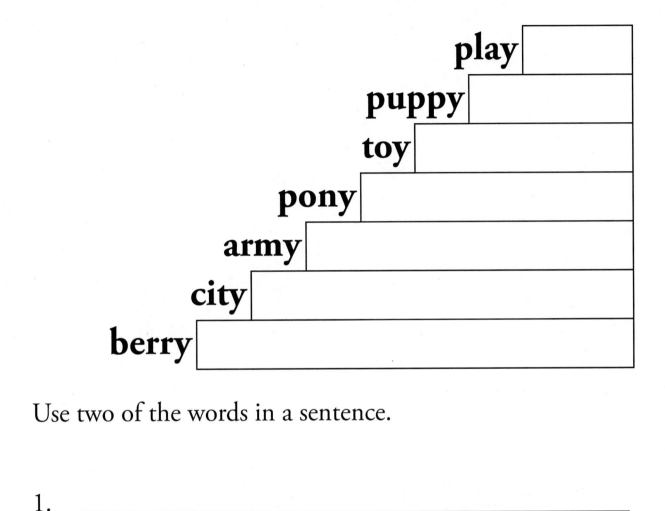

Use two of the words in a sentence.

1. _____

_____

_____

_____

The Visit

Directions: Have students read the story "The Visit" and answer the questions in complete sentences.

1. What is Mrs. Gunter's job?

   _____

   _____

   _____

2. Kim hails a cab. What is a synonym for cab?

   _____

   _____

   _____

3. What does riding fast in the cab make Kurt think of?

   _____

   _____

   _____

4. What are some risks of driving too fast?

   _____

   _____

   _____

5. What do you think a paycheck is?

_____

_____

_____

6. What are the Gunters going to do to celebrate Kim's getting a job?

_____

_____

_____

7. When Kim tells Mrs. Gunter that Kurt ate a lot, what does Mrs. Gunter say?

_____

_____

_____

Battery Park

1. Where are the Gunters picnicking?

    _____

    _____

    _____

2. What does Kurt think the Statue of Liberty is holding in her hand?

    _____

    _____

    _____

3. What is the Statue of Liberty really holding?

    _____

    _____

    _____

Directions: Have students read the story and answer the questions in complete sentences.

4. Who gave the Statue of Liberty to the people of the United States?

_____

_____

_____

5. What is the largest present you've ever gotten?

_____

_____

_____

6. What does liberty mean?

_____

_____

_____

1. How did Kim feel after she got her job?

2. What was Mrs. Gunter's job?

3. What color was the cab?

4. How did the driver know where to go?

5. How did the cab man drive?

6. Did the cab driver have a license?

7. What did Mrs. Gunter do when she saw Kim?

8. What places did Kim list?

9. What did Kim use to help her get her job?

10. What impressed Mr. Fremont?

Directions: Using the story "The Visit" on Worksheet PP45, have students underline the answer to each question and write the question number in the margin beside the text.

1. Kurt and Kim took a cab to see Mrs. Gunter.

2. Kurt is scared during the cab ride.

3. The Gunter family members like to give hugs.

4. Mrs. Gunter was proud of Kim.

5. Kim was surprised at the kind of job that she got.

The Visit

Kim was happy that she had found herself a summer job.

"Let's go and visit Mom," she said. "She will be finished teaching by the time we get there."

Mrs. Gunter was a math teacher. She taught at a college in lower Manhattan.

Kim held up a hand to hail a cab.

A yellow cab screeched to a stop on the side of the street. Kurt and Kim hopped in.

"Where to?" asked the driver.

Kim told him the address.

The cab went shooting off. Wind came rushing in the windows as the cab sped past stores on both sides.

Kurt hung on tight. It was a crazy ride. The cab man was weaving in and out of traffic. Kurt thought they might crash. Part of him was frightened. But part of him found driving at that speed exciting. It was like riding in a race car.

"Do you have a license to drive?" Kurt called to the driver.

"Yes. All cab drivers must have a license," the driver said.

"And they teach you to drive like this?"

"No, no," said the driver. "It takes years and years of driving to become an expert like me!"

They made it safely. Kim paid the driver and gave him a tip. She and Kurt went in to see their mom.

Mrs. Gunter gave Kim a big hug. Kurt snuck in between them so he could be part of the hug, too. Then Kim told her mom how they had spent the day.

Kim listed the places they had visited. She explained what had happened with Tom and Beth, with Alberto at the Corner Market, with Dwight, the

Man of Light, with Hester the Florist, and, at last, with Mr. Fremont. She told her mom how she had used math to help her get the job at the grocery.

By the end of the story, Mrs. Gunter was beaming. "You see," she said. "I told you math would help you out one day. You thought I was crazy."

"You were right," said Kim. "Mr. Fremont was really impressed that I could add up the tally without the cash register and also add in the sales tax."

"Good for you!" said her mom. "I'm so proud of you!"

"I never dreamed I would have a job in a grocery," added Kim, "but I think it's going to be a good job for me."

"It may not be the job of your dreams," said her mom. "But it's a job. The next job you get can be better. And the next one can be even better. If you study hard in college, you will have a chance to get the job of your dreams some day. Until then, just do a good job and save as much of your paycheck as you can."

"I will," said Kim.

"Let's do something fun!" said Kurt.

"I know!" said their mom. "Let's celebrate Kim's getting a job by getting some subs and snacks and going down to Battery Park for a picnic. Are you two hungry for dinner?"

"You bet!" said Kurt.

"This is crazy!" Kim said. "Mom, all day, Kurt ate and ate. Each time I got him a snack, I said, that's the end of that. But he was still hungry."

"Well, he's a strong, growing child," said Mrs. Gunter. "And he was busy all day."

"That's right!" said Kurt.

They went to a sub shop nearby. Mrs. Gunter ordered a sub for each of them, plus some snacks and drinks.

Then Mrs. Gunter hailed a cab. The three of them got in. The cab took them down the West Side Highway. It dropped them off in Battery Park, on the south end of Manhattan.

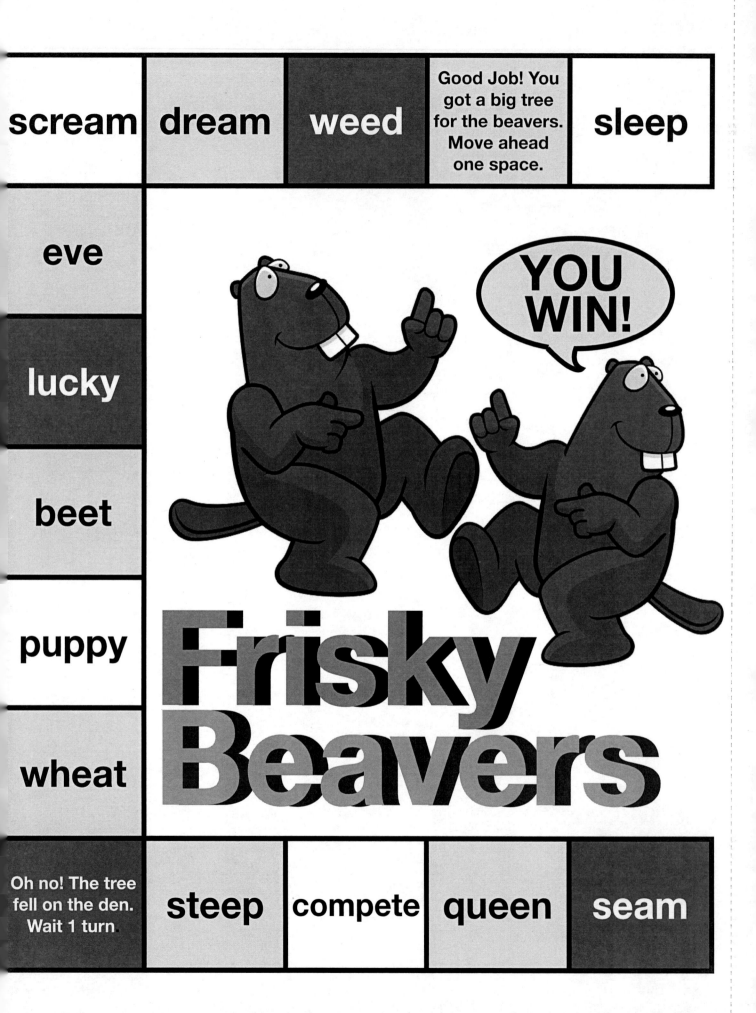

athlete	steamy	eat	glee	**START**
		streak		greedy
tree	jelly	stream		Oops! You fell in the pond. Dry off and wait one turn.
		happy		deed
		teeth		Pete
		mean		beam
creek	silly	green	team	cheap

Frisky Beavers
/ee/

Directions: Have students throw the die to move a game piece. Students will read the word in the space, then write the word in the correct column on this sheet. See Pausing Point in the Teacher Guide for alternate ways to play and win.

'e_e'	'ea'	'ee'	'y'

CORE KNOWLEDGE LANGUAGE ARTS

SERIES EDITOR-IN-CHIEF
E. D. Hirsch, Jr.

PRESIDENT
Linda Bevilacqua

EDITORIAL STAFF
Carolyn Gosse, Senior Editor - Preschool
Khara Turnbull, Materials Development Manager
Michelle L. Warner, Senior Editor - Listening & Learning

Mick Anderson
Robin Blackshire
Maggie Buchanan
Paula Coyner
Sue Fulton
Sara Hunt
Erin Kist
Robin Luecke
Rosie McCormick
Cynthia Peng
Liz Pettit
Ellen Sadler
Deborah Samley
Diane Auger Smith
Sarah Zelinke

DESIGN AND GRAPHICS STAFF
Scott Ritchie, Creative Director

Kim Berrall
Michael Donegan
Liza Greene
Matt Leech
Bridget Moriarty
Lauren Pack

CONSULTING PROJECT MANAGEMENT SERVICES
ScribeConcepts.com

ADDITIONAL CONSULTING SERVICES
Ang Blanchette
Dorrit Green
Carolyn Pinkerton

ACKNOWLEDGMENTS

These materials are the result of the work, advice, and encouragement of numerous individuals over many years. Some of those singled out here already know the depth of our gratitude; others may be surprised to find themselves thanked publicly for help they gave quietly and generously for the sake of the enterprise alone. To helpers named and unnamed we are deeply grateful.

CONTRIBUTORS TO EARLIER VERSIONS OF THESE MATERIALS
Susan B. Albaugh, Kazuko Ashizawa, Nancy Braier, Kathryn M. Cummings, Michelle De Groot, Diana Espinal, Mary E. Forbes, Michael L. Ford, Ted Hirsch, Danielle Knecht, James K. Lee, Diane Henry Leipzig, Martha G. Mack, Liana Mahoney, Isabel McLean, Steve Morrison, Juliane K. Munson, Elizabeth B. Rasmussen, Laura Tortorelli, Rachael L. Shaw, Sivan B. Sherman, Miriam E. Vidaver, Catherine S. Whittington, Jeannette A. Williams

We would like to extend special recognition to Program Directors Matthew Davis and Souzanne Wright who were instrumental to the early development of this program.

SCHOOLS
We are truly grateful to the teachers, students, and administrators of the following schools for their willingness to field test these materials and for their invaluable advice: Capitol View Elementary, Challenge Foundation Academy (IN), Community Academy Public Charter School, Lake Lure Classical Academy, Lepanto Elementary School, New Holland Core Knowledge Academy, Paramount School of Excellence, Pioneer Challenge Foundation Academy, New York City PS 26R (The Carteret School), PS 30X (Wilton School), PS 50X (Clara Barton School), PS 96Q, PS 102X (Joseph O. Loretan), PS 104Q (The Bays Water), PS 214K (Michael Friedsam), PS 223Q (Lyndon B. Johnson School), PS 308K (Clara Cardwell), PS 333Q (Goldie Maple Academy), Sequoyah Elementary School, South Shore Charter Public School, Spartanburg Charter School, Steed Elementary School, Thomas Jefferson Classical Academy, Three Oaks Elementary, West Manor Elementary.

And a special thanks to the CKLA Pilot Coordinators Anita Henderson, Yasmin Lugo-Hernandez, and Susan Smith, whose suggestions and day-to-day support to teachers using these materials in their classrooms was critical.